MW00615699

certain birds

poems

Thomas R. Peters, Jr.

î

Elik Press
Salt Lake City 2012

Also by Thomas R. Peters, Jr.:

Listen to My Machine

100 missed train stations

Over the roofs of the world

The Book of Silence

I know why the caged bird drinks
       (with Jack Collom & others)

For my teachers: Allen, Anne, Andrei, Diane,
Ed, Harry, Jack, Jim, Gregory, Peter, Reed, Robert, Stan,
Susan & William

& for my mom Lillian, my sisters Jennifer & Sarah
Jeanne & my niece Caroline, my aunt Margery & my
grandmothers Nona & Mimi

& for Alexandra, Allison, Ashley, Becca, Caitlin, Cindy,
Deborah, Erin, Euphrosyne, Jennifer, Kamala, Katherine,
Lauren, Lindsay, Mary, Rebecca, Susan, Suzanne
(Shoshanna) & Ula . . .

& Andy & Rose, Matt & Sarah, Chris Dyer, Darrin &
Karin, Tyler & Vanessa & Daron & Jim Cohn for their
kind understanding & patience during the various stages
of publishing my books, & Randy Roark for continual
help copy editing my work.

First Printing
First Edition

Cover art: Tom Peters and Nicholas Motte

Peters, Jr., Thomas R.
    certain birds: poems / Thomas R. Peters, Jr.

ISBN-13   978-0-9818567-0-4
ISBN-10   0-9818567-0-5

Some of these poems appeared in various journals, including *Anatomy Raw*, *The Bolinas Hearsay News*, *Make Room for Dada*, *The Red Moon Review*, *The Exqusite Corpse*, *The Hawaii Review*, *In This Corner*, *The New Censorship*, and in the anthology *Poems from Penny Lane*. "The Book of Silence" appeared as a Left Hand Chapbook. Thanks to the editors of these and forgotten publications.

elikpress.com

certain birds

life

a beautiful
girl walking
down the
street

complaining.

life in the 21st century

a beautiful
woman walking
down the
street

complaining
on her
cell phone.

"I drank for many years
   and then I died."
                    Scott Fitz
      "she puts camels out in milk"
                    Jeffrey Miller

I had a serious bout
w/ Alcoholism
Mike Tyson
socking me in
the head with
a Budweiser
bottle

A bottle in
one mouth
& a Kerouac
in the other.
I couldn't
pay the rent
at the
Alcohol
Recovery
Center of the
mind.

I serve drinks
across the
morning bar
to Alcoholics
in my image
a toothless

smile &
fifty cent
tip in the
brown sunshine,
reflecting
off the carpet
27 miles
below my
shoes.

No Dice for the Zen Buddhists

I lit another Export A
with the butt of my last one
& put it out in my Spumoni,
when some shadowy religious soul
stepped up to my table & exclaimed,
"I know you can obliterate the ego,"
when I responded "why don't you
forge your way out the door, asshole
& make some shadows,"
they formed a circle
around me, but being
the elusive type, I disappeared
into a pile of ashes
on the bar stool.

Tennis

everything
is a poem
to me, even
prose, she sd
hitting the ball
over the fence

James Agee
died on
the tennis court,
he sd
"who was
he playing
John Ashbery?"
No, John
Huston,
he died
of a
stroke.

Really Starting Something

she had the attraction
powers of 12 gross bottles of musk,
unopened no less & shined
with a fiery incandescence
that inspired even the homeless
to get jobs, we were at
serious risk of getting
perpendicular & then she
declared that her yeast
infection was inflamed
& intercourse was out
of the question, something
more kinky was in order
& it took a svelte sensibility,
the rest was all a soup
of human juices & egos
& some things should
be left to the imagination.

a million miles away (I want you)

Hey, you gnarled my heart
& left me forsaken in the sack
I was anxious of the silence, tumbling
in your hair, tell me you raging fuck,
your love is like tofu at McDonalds
as original as a happy face, babe
I'm in love with obsequies bugs
passionate like colored prophylactics
why not? It's like Julie Andrews
singing about halitosis and other
unpronounceable things, my heart,
passionate like angry sex, ugly
like tying your dog to a truck
I'm sick of Valentine's Day, already.

a small but seminal way
in September

What can I do on
a night like this;
laundry, talk on
the telephone to an
old friend who once
froze his dead cat
in a plastic bag in
our freezer, who
wants to know what
we will do now when
he visits, since I've quit
drinking, watch the
Little Rascals on TV,
go to the 7-11 for
an egg roll, cashews,
an avocado & cream
cheese sandwich
& a lottery ticket, read,
"A poem for trapped
things," & a moth flies
through the bathroom
curtains, lands on my
back, my leg, with
brown transparent
wings, scratch the scar
on my right hand
& the moth flies out
the window into
the September air.

In the Morning with Suede Trousers

Lying there amongst the gardenias
I was overcome with infatuation
the thermometer had since exploded
like some cartoon,
& I was contemplating death
(in the Shakespearean sense)
& with a murmur
she crawled over to me
like ants to a peony
& we made love like anarchists
throwing convention aside,
the next morning I awoke
feeling swampy
& exhausted like a man
living on a diet of potatoes
(too much starch)
barely able to pull on
my suede trousers,
I slipped away.

The White Cop
for Apollinaire

the angels sing & the angels
dance in my heart
but not in the police officer's
across the street

his blue uniform shines
& ruins my Christmas
his badge glistens in the sun
destroying my heart

I would like to shove
a bunch of flowers up his ass
& reign snow on his grave
as delicate as tiny bras.

One down, eight to go

The shortest distance
between two points
is around the block
which you call your
heart, turkey buzzards
swoon at the thought
of the little death that
melts you into an
ice cream stain on
my sheets, chequered
by the past.
    I spontaneously
combust with your love,
like bubbles on the
pavement & have but
nine lives to spend
inside you.

Death Rock

At the dance
hall, my friend's
Puerto Rican girlfriend,
Terry, asked me, "how are
things going?" "Miserable,"
I responded. "Why?" "My girlfriend and I broke up
& she lives next door."
"Is it terminal?" she asked.
She meant permanent.
"Yes," it was terminal
some part of me
had just died.

Delirium
  after Arthur Rimbaud

15 minutes 'til the matinee, my sweet
the summer of love revisited
my beer evaporates in the sun
as we stare at the dirty hippies

The Bass dance in the vast sunlight
burning like Hesperus
Yesterday's agitants in shirts of cotton
looking like "The Carpenters"

we dance silently as pudding
as they slaughter
the lamb
on the hill
for the fifth time

O, we say goodbye little charmers
subjects of Babylon
Venus would quit in an instant
at the site of these lame children

maybe if it rained hamburgers
these gypsies would
leave us in peace
to attend to our afternoon swim.

Adventures in a Wax Museum

Vincent Price was looking
very Glam

& pondering sex
with the dead

a scared union

in the sand
with a wax figure
of Paulette Goddard,

violent sex meant
nothing to the porpoise
said John Lilly, they
were always compassionate,
but to the B-movie stars
there was no alternative
it burned inside like cold fire.

Cinema Automatique
for Apollinaire

the children are either dead
or dancing at the movie theatre

they enjoy their death
these children of vile women
seeming bourgeois with
their imported cigarettes

& Catholic burials
the music is vile
& the nuances of the heart
commenced like barbed wire

the movie was over
& they charged out like Romans
crushing each other
with perfect symmetry
their souls rise out
of my beer glass
with a murmur
like neon.

Ode to Her Purple Doc Martens
for ashley

slender
with sixty-four eyelets
they'd make anyone
forget the phrase
"your Mother wears combat boots,"
lovely arch with thick
crepe rubber soles
careening up to her
flawless kneesocks
makes me shiver
& trip
uh oh!
I melt
like water
on the wicked witch
of the west or a single
framed film of a candle
dripping off my chair
like molten metal
leaving a pile
of ash.

summer's almost gone or
a hunka-hunka burninglove

In the frothy morning
the icicles were melting
& I was spreading cheez whiz
on melba toast with both hands
"I'm ambidextrous, see!"
then she walked by all willowy
subtly undulating
in her elephantine blue
jean bell bottoms—
She was a fashion plate
I was conspiring to her smile
her teeth sparkled like white amethysts
& I was swimming in desire
lost like a wombat in Montana.

I conspire like a wombat

Her love was willowy
& ambidextrous
& she undulated
all subtle and frothy
when I saw her I froze
like an icicle
hard as an amethyst
I felt better than a case
of cheez whiz
& a pile of
fashion magazines.

One after Raymond Queneau & two others

I.
What have I
been given
two feet to walk on
a language
a species to continue
one small morsel of a
civilization
to devour,
"the human conscious"

II.
is it the function
of the past to dwell
in the sky
& swim in a
moment of language.

III.
What has become
of my faculties
this sentimental intelligence
is one large volume,
a check written
in moderation
to the human family,
but what audible body
will spend one blond decade
dancing with the humans
who will find satisfaction
only in death.

Dear Jim, it's 1:45 pm
my cat Villon is at the doctor
Peter is on the loose, it is not
the year of parrot fever, my dream
was the class being interesting
the Academy of Fairview is closing
its doors, the only famous women
who went here are famous for their
beauty is not what they teach here
Dear Jim, it's not 1953 the Year of
Bwana Devil, it's 1995 the year
that sounds like a bargain price
my dream is to sleep all day & dream,
it's 1:50 pm the day is almost over

Dear Jim, it's 1:45 pm, the sonnets
are writing themselves, Peter is on the loose
In my dream there was a plane crash
It was the year of union control
Nikita Khrushchev & Robert E. Lee
have taken over Penny Lane, it's
the year of pierced everything
Dear Jim, it's not 1953 the Year
of the Bwana Devil, it's 1995
the year that sounds like a bargain
price, my dream is to sleep all day
& dream, it's 1:50 pm the day's almost
over, the Academy of Fairbanks is
opening its doors, Hello it's time

Clare A. Voyance

We aim to please the passing choirs
as they charge through the mosque
in their burgundy camaros, thinking
of Duluth & the danger of falling into
                                    the sad Lake Superior

& her fantastic undergarments,
trout are singing in the ice cream mirror
of love that lives on the street of vanquished
                                    opportunity
the air doesn't matter to the Iroquois rating
buttons with their hats made of bells

St. Clair is calm and the moon is in love with the
beautiful rivers that dance ecstatic in sunglasses
the jet pilots are large as they explode in
the penniless sky filled with marbles

Saint Clair

Shut up Amy & move those chairs
I want you in a charming mask in the beer
garden
or dancing with a latté like some quasi
Tristan Tzara writhing fantastic under the sun

or Take off out to sea like some minor
in love with vain opportunity
unable to pass by, the air is full of rime
& Laurie chases me through the meleé

(by the light of the moon)

Oh to have you in a calm tryst would be
more beautiful than fainting over olives
or dancing in front of the television
with wraparound sunglasses

do you exist like jetplanes
in the orange sky exploding
above while we play marbles

We lost a lot of good ones in July

Dear Em, it's 9:15 & I'm
not Ted Berrigan or Jeffrey
Miller (for that matter) it's a
shitty job smoking cigar-
ettes & listening to planes
flying overhead, we're above
ground & there's no cream for
my Folgers. I'd like to stretch
my canvas from here to Denver
because the cradle of civilization
is somewhere between the STYRO
warehouse & THREEWIT COOPER
    I have Atlantic City tattooed
on my chest, Dear Mark, it's
9:23 I have Arthur Rimbaud
painted on my toenails & I'm
gonna spend my summer driving
Exquisite Corpses to
Surrealist Film Festivals.

IOWA IN

we wait for the day

& it comes

chasing the dawn

for two eggs,

a tumbleweed &

"The New York Times,"

the semis around

here carry tractors

to pull us out of

this mess, we join

their drivers

for a cup of coffee

& the poets in Lynnville

write about fields

& the barns sagging,

while we weep

over bacon

& Interstates.

POETRY DRIVES YOU CRAZY

Poetry drives you crazy
at this time of morning
I know because I'm reading
poetry now & I am crazy.
"I started reading poetry
because I hated My Religion."
"Why did you hate Merrill Lynch,
was your Dad a stockbroker
or something?" Poetry can drive
you crazy at this time of morning. I know because I'm drunk,
I always get drunk when I drink
all night at this time of morning.

after Kyger, after de Angulo, after

Coyote man
        felt bad
when the first man died
        he wanted to
bring him back

Meadowlark said
        Men smell they're
better off dead

Coyote said
        they smell worse
dead, meadowlark

Oh yeah,
        said Meadowlark.

Poem with 1st stanza written
by Frank O'Hara in a dream

I wait for her

like a wave
that crashes

(at the back
 of her neck)

it crashes
I wait for her

being apart
gnaws at me
like a bobcat
biting off
its foot stuck
in a trap,
I'm stuck here
in my bed.

And it Echoes

She had the
emotional range of
an abstract expressionist
an endless car-horn
sounding off
the Zelda Fitzgerald
of modern dance
made me want to
take up golf again
drive balls against
the monotony –
Oh, Frank O'Hara sd
it all but we must
go on living,
loving, remaining
in the background,
like movie stars
amidst all that glorious
poverty, sleeping late
& drinking whenever we
wanted to – There are
a thousand free movies
at the library & all
those books, "imagine!"

Girl Crazy

This morning
1991, riding
my $200 dollar motor-
cycle, listening
to Viva Las Vegas (50 cents)
on my $2.50 Walkman,
I wonder who it was
that asked, "How could've
Elvis had so much fun
in the movies on
a bus boy's wage?"

"The men don't know,
but the little girls understand."

Sometimes California
is more beautiful than
a mushroom omelet
on a freezing morning,
like this one, I keep
running into the same
women, but they're with
different guys, every day.

My horrible childhood
is coming back to haunt me

The coffee shops
in San Francisco
are decorated
like Pee-wee's Playhouse
& used bell bottoms
cost $80.
The clerk in
Platforms stands
in front of
a Starsky & Hutch
poster, this 70s
nostalgia has gone
far enough.

In the translucent morning

sitting under
a tree, pondering
turtles
I suddenly smelled
croissants
in the fragrant
air
no difference
between plastic
& sterling
flowing

translucency sonnet

sitting under
a tree, pondering
the turtles flowing
by, the fragrance
of croissants—
sends my thoughts
off thinking of
sterling tea services
in the plastic morning
no time for juice
have to run

past the flowing
morning sterling

"truth is zebra
running through
a white birch forest"
            anonymous

her poems
were so good
you'd always
find pubic hairs
between
the pages
of her books

Zen & the Birds of Appetite

after too many
cups of espresso
I left my body
for deep space,
I had to piss like
a dog, found the nearest
tree indigenous to this
part of the country,
just as I was getting ready
for my leakage, I spotted
two pygmies frolicking
in the flesh & tyrone power
looking very much like a circus geek
biting the heads off chickens,
I felt like I was in the film,
"Nightmare Alley," it must've
been all that Limburger
cheese I ate.

advice
to the pretty
girl on
her
cell phone

hang up

the moon over Africa

the moon will rise
over Africa tomorrow
now it sits like
a hat on the horizon,
clouds still visible,
these plants that dress
up the earth
thriving off melted
snow & rain,
I personally am
heartbroken about
running over a
porcupine &
seek shelter
in the folds
of your dress.

The Persistence of Memory
    "I is another"
        Arthur Rimbaud

I used to be a lunch pail
but now I am the cafeteria.

I used to be the bus to school
but now I am the school itself.

I used to be Generalissimo Francisco Franco
but now I'm Bozo the clown.

I used to be a covered wagon
but now I'm a forties pump.

I used to be a horseradish
but now I'm an encyclopedia.

I used to be Dali's mustache
but now I'm a razor blade.

I used to be forgetfulness
but now I'm tomorrow.

What I Remember from Lisa Jarnot's Reading
for L.J.

At the meridian
where I saw the bird
near the meridian
at at at the corner
of Sixth by a side street
where I saw Lou Reed
the meridian
at the meridian
where I saw the bird
in Jane & Anselm's backyard
at the meridian
where I saw the bird
the meridian
Hockey Night in Canada
are the Stars really playing tonight?
scowl
swish swish swish
corduroy scowl
at the meridian
it's such an honor
with Bernadette Mayer
behind me
at the meridian
the bird
scarf
the bird
did I start at 8:25
are the Sabres really playing tonight?
Buffalo
Hockey night in Jane & Anselm's backyard
do you recognize it?

Nam Rats God
  for Stan Brakhage

1.
Above the little
        do not worry
cared little to leave the house
        come with us
To fell the sacred top!
        Obeying
He grabbed an axe
        Made the long climb, slowly
The only tree there
        a bowman
the goddess herself shot,
        looked down
shall touch the ground
        their cottage
swung an axe for the slanting
        while they wondered
the oak tree trembled
        seeing the neighbors trouble
And acorns paled
        and the poor quarters
And when the axe bit into
        me a temple
As from the neck
        to the marble columns;
And they were all stunned;
        the root was golden
And they paid for their devotion
        with this carefully carved
axe of Eurystheus
        struck marble

II.
Then turning to them
till, from death the other
most dear to favor
and my final prophecy:
in my hour of death, little?
This did not stop him either
weakened by blows, dragged down
like to be fell,
and its falling weight
laid low the temple

For ten miles around and the dry years
together
stunned at their own, their forest neither
Robed all in black; per se
punished by seeing
they prayed, from
the beautiful, was granted
made the fields tremble
    watched the temple
She planned an awful punishment
    for the mortals
was something days over
in any act of his; she would cut loaves
appeal to famine they still had time
Are never allowed to meet
and the bark was closed over
Summoned one of the mountains
            even to this day.

"Almost every trace of the Moths"
with Jack Spicer

I.
With the gums gone you
are toothless, And the nose is next to nothing
the eye alive

And now the rattling
Of the radiator   the floor
is loose, the even row of it
fit to raise 11 children.

You will count on them 1, 2, 4, 8, One hundred
You will stay in the midst of them,
You will know them, you will hear them
in the narrow meadow

II.
In the endless endlessness
snow, sea salt
He lost his teeth

Without eyes or thumbs
He suffers from restlessness
How to lick a wound
          (salt)
His lover left.

Snow sea salt love
In the lovely endlessness

III.
Blue rooted heron, loon lake
river song, like me no traveler
taking a rest, loose-winged water-bird
And dumb with music theory.

I stand upon the waterfront,
like him no traveler
before, dangling on Icarus wings

Aching for flight, for waxen wings
I ache and take my rest

So let us die for death alone is motion
And death alone will make these herons fly.
I fall wingless in the ocean
& die.

Meanwhile Back at the Ranch

I was feeling inspired
so I made myself a drink & turned on the TV
I don't think there's anything
I like more than more than
Modern Poetry & cartoons
except for Vodka & film noir
or watching you get dressed in the morning,
you say, how do you make yourself a drink?
just what turns on a TV?
this morning, I read the lives of
Auden, Corso, Sexton & Ed Dorn,
"No one that followed her poetry
was surprised when she committed
suicide in 1974,"
How much longer shall I inhabit
the lower east side
this weekend I looked for Gregory
at the "kettle of fish,"
Auden at the Holiday Bar.

Morning television sucks,
so do the guys outside with the jackhammers,
at 5am I heard a car window crash
followed by a car alarm which drove away,
Rimbaud lived to the ripe old age of 37
he didn't die at 19 he just stopped
living, HENRI de TOULOUSE-LAUTREC
made a painting in 1896 that looks
so much like Caitlin, it's called
"Femme a' sa toilette,"
Woman Dressing, that
I had to draw

a tattoo on her back
now they no longer resemble
each other,

In the last few weeks
I've traveled thousands
of miles on trains,
in two days my niece
Caroline will be one year old,
some day she will
understand this,
I hope by then
I will too.

Let Freedom Ring
            "at this time we hope you feel
                free to stay tuned for instructional
                programming"

My high school history teacher
used to say to me,
"What did you see on your trip,
   the inside of some bars?"
he was usually right
this week things are back to usual
this country like "we" found it,
the Braves are kicking the Indians' ass,
Betty Page is dancing with a chair
on the same TV I saw a symphony
of mice the night before,
some guy with fishnets & platforms
is singing about living on a chinese rock
& another guy with a necklace made of cows'
teeth
& long fingernails dressed in black leather
from head to toe with a snakeskin
hatband just bought me a drink,
the painting of Carl Sandburg above
the bar reminds me of Jeff
on another wall "blockhead,"
is pounding a nail into his nose
with a hammer, the bartender
who used to serve Auden
in his pajamas shows me his
1940s soccer clippings,

the cab driver who told
us his wife's full lips
were like kissing a rare roast beef
shows us her picture
& she's beautiful

My Prayer

Caitlin, full of Grace

daughter

of the son

of the father

of the underworld

lover

of those

not assembled

in one room

amongst women

blessed is me

who

is left

waiting at

the end of the line

blessed is you

amongst aimees

chelseas, lylas

annes & emilys

blessed is you

at the lesbian ball

amongst the bards

not at college

empowered amongst women

with lots of pubic hair

not impregnated by love

but spirits

poems between leaves

of salmon

in the copper canyons

amongst the Sam Hamills

& Suzan Alparslans

needing something

shiny & metallic

involving muscles & birth

divining wisdom

at random

from old dictionaries

found on a bench

besides

long island

the cape

port townsend

san francisco

once a landlocked

child - somewhere

between virginity

& justice

brought up

amongst women

on a hill

fourteen streets

from a mountain

9 X 22

1969's ok

won't you bring me a

moment

of your time

amongst the

garden & the flowers

where we can't

tell the difference

between Leonard Cohen

& our telephone

conversation

It's 4 in the morning

but I'm afraid

it's not December

the music Bill Clinton

likes is hard to remember

I know I'm not

your brother your killer

I once had a phone

sincerely, Al Capone

or something like that

the mountains

full of mist

I walked through

with you have

transformed

from Dublin to Kyoto

every person

must have a dog

to walk down

this path trodden

by people in uniform

sleeping has

become impossible

with you without you

it's really

the garbage & the flowers

in the dumpster

behind the flower market

& no one's ever

brought me tea

or oranges

or anything

from China

I'd settle

for your orange

hair in my crook

on a summer night

with no hope

of fall interrupting

amongst you

a woman

full of grace

with me

a man.

The Book of Silence

In my dream they asked

if anyone would like to read

with Diane di Prima.

I raised my hand.

You need multiple Ph.D's

to be taken seriously.

"Men talking about feminism

is like the deaf signing

about music," she said.

It is possible, I responded.

Young man, You have to

make it a surprise,

as long as it is out of

this world.

They kept referring back

to the language of the birds,

"The hopes of my life

are bound up in him"

Hey, Ho

the lark

& the owl!

The path of the

bird annihilates east

& west.

In the grove the

fallen leaves

are many.

You have to break

out in song,

invoked by a band of

armed dancers,

with the cult of the

Creeleys at Black Mountain,

the ritual of

the minstrels

are numberless,

I vow to

kill the foetus,

the angry messiahs

with no hope of this

world, went out in the air to wail

and become elegant

but we don't have to go there

It has to do with knowing

every time a poet puts

down two words

you split into two,

the bishop & the tomb

dividing the line,

slowing down enough to draw

from a deeper place

with a line or two

that can lead somewhere

away from the water

where you have been

the other voices go.

I've been watching

your captors

They do not labor anymore

in the human crucible.

water into will

down, down.

we visit the interior

where things are not disturbed

sitting watching you dance

in happy hours,

in vegetable silver,

in the growing erotic tensions

across distances

by Mother Goose.

you like it

by the side of the phone,

we discuss an issue

in a voice that commands attention

like a Greek chorus

affected by a speech

given by the opposite sex

or the mystics around,

trusting your insights,

who invented

a magic jar

with no air inside it

only knowledge that's readily available

& in search of prey

by mail

& the notion of tribe

in the presence of Hermes

who makes sounds that

we make,

like the thing

that is signed by the

sign & the emptiness of the

sign instead of romantic hypothesis

a semiotic code

like an exact reproduction of the

upside-down mode of language

with its roots in heaven

like the child coming up with

sentences that he's never heard

spontaneous order

arises

like heat death

or entropy & accident,

the nature of chaos

gives rise to form

like sudden change

forsaken like basketball

for art or space,

the embryo a being

with nothing to say

except that chaos is embryotic

form,

giving rise

to the first gods

the antithesis of divine frivolity

like the dance

originating from the lack of space

lying between language and seduction

its orphic qualities

bringing order out of childhood

making us two out of

the languages invented by children,

organs invented out of intuition

like the wolf children

taken out of the forest

before they are allowed to speak,

words beneath words

an infinite pattern of echoes and repetitions

imbedded in language.

Hawk gods carrying

us away from language without death

moving us closer to things

that resemble themselves,

arcane like streetcleaners at 4 am

in Hermetic week,

opposites complementary

in the river

that precedes the universe

we view as complimentary,

an eleventh wing,

unfinished, they are out of the egg,

wanting to be scholars

throwing dictionary definitions around

for two years

taking out your eyes if you wrote

about yourself

or anything giving

information about horses

or ideal nature

as in the hiding place for the hare,

preceded by forlorn hope

or form;

giving up all hope of forlorn logic,

the basis of all fiction

giving rise to questions of meter,

inventing new forms,

a chronology of memory

about forty feet long

& five feet high,

not relating to structure

remembering the green couch

on the previous page

or how to deal with commas,

as the present gets closer,

never seeing this much with your eyes,

precisely the unnameable,

words with no cause but themselves

that glow on blades,

fade and disappear

merely more weary than yesterday,

a tense intelligence

as dead as music

when it was first sounded

with long black pauses

like Beethoven's 7th Symphony,

a whisper of final music

I tried to understand,

like the language of the birds,

a pell-mell silence

in which the grown-ups pursued me

in lieu of particulars

symbolized by themselves,

sitting in the corner of the grove

elongated by the wild

beast language of the Futurists,

a game of repetition

baffling referentiality,

separating form from content

without allowing it to rest,

almost like the thinking of the dying,

a diagram of illusion,

the business of looking back

at the extreme structure

of future lyric,

cigarettes smoking

in the wind.

.

26

d

Elik Press Singles
Michael Ortiz Hill, *Blues Song at the Edge of Chaos*
Michael Ortiz Hill & Deena Metzger,
   Sacred Illness, Sacred Medicine
Michael Ortiz Hill & Deena Metzger,
   Meeting Sacred Illness
Deena Metzger, *Living the Ritual*
Craig Bernardini & Tanya Radford,
   Your Street is Not Your Street Anymore
Anne Waldman, *Manifestos*
Anne Waldman, *Radical Presence*
Anne Waldman, *War Crime*
Ernesto Cardenal, *Revolution/Evolution*
Steve Creson, *The Occult of Not Seeing*
William Burroughs, *You Cant Win*
Allen Ginsberg, *Dont Fuck Up Your Revolution*
Andy Hoffmann, *Dante in Mexico*
Andy Hoffmann, *Beck Street*
Michael Gills, *Tomb Angels*
Jim Jones, *Kerouac in Seattle*
Jim Jones, *Carl Solomon: Report from the Sane Asylum*
Paul West, *Samuel Beckett, Born Astride a Grave*
Paul West, *The Backlash Against the Novel*
Jeff Metcalf, *The Last Steelhead*
Michael Adams, *Between Heaven & Earth*

Elik Poetry Series
Hector Ahumada, *The Highland Travelers/Los*
   Viajeros del Altiplano
Randy Roark, *The San Francisco Notebook*
Ira Cohen, *Chaos & Glory*
Joel Long, *Chopins Preludes*
Alex Caldiero, *Body/Dreams/Organs*
K.W. Brewer, *Chiaroscuro*
John Sinclair, *full moon night*
Ira Cohen, *Gods Bounty*
Jeffrey Taylor, *dont put it in your mouth*
Hector Ahumada, *Earth and Air Poems/Poemas*
   Tierra y Aire
Joel Long, *Saffron Beneath Every Frost*

Elik: one who has eyes